W9-DFT-290

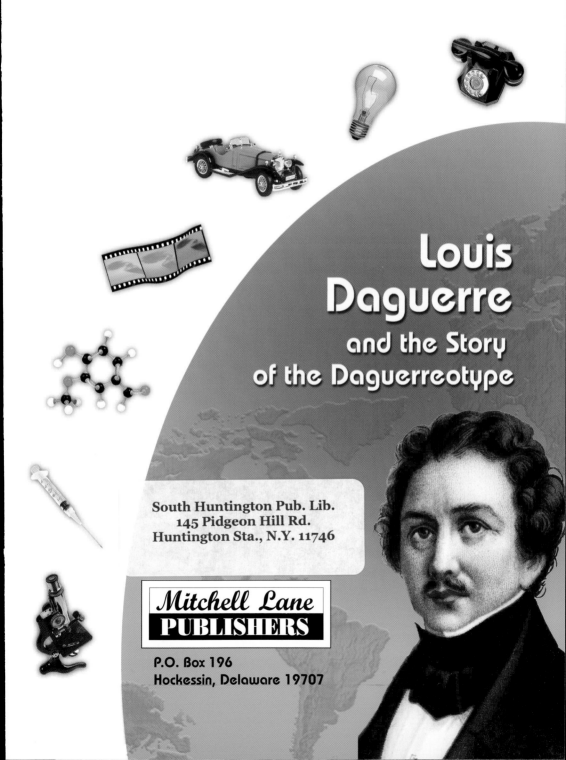

Uncharted, Unexplored, and Unexplained

Scientific Advancements of the 19th Century

Louis Daguerre
and the Story of the Daguerreotype

Mitchell Lane
PUBLISHERS

P.O. Box 196
Hockessin, Delaware 19707

Uncharted, Unexplored, and Unexplained

Scientific Advancements of the 19th Century

Visit us on the web: www.mitchelllane.com
Comments? email us: mitchelllane@mitchelllane.com

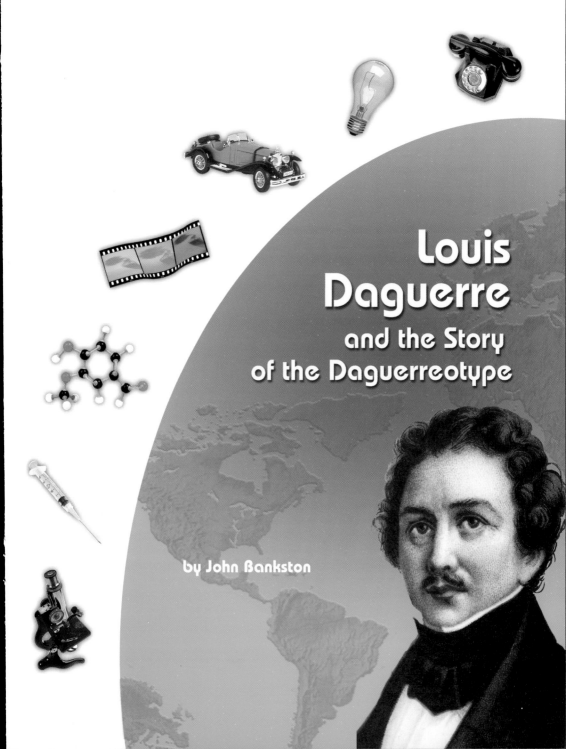

Louis Daguerre
and the Story of the Daguerreotype

by John Bankston

Uncharted, Unexplored, and Unexplained

Scientific Advancements of the 19th Century

Mitchell Lane
PUBLISHERS

Printing   2   3   4   5   6   7   8
        Library of Congress Cataloging-in-Publication Data
Bankston, John, 1974-
      Louis Daguerre and the daguerreotype / John Bankston.
        p. cm. — (Uncharted, unexplored & unexplained)
Includes bibliographical references and index.
      ISBN 1-58415-247-8
      1. Photography—History—Juvenile literature. 2. Daguerre, Louis Jacques Mandé, 1787-1851—Juvenile literature. 3. Daguerreotype—History—Juvenile literature. [1. Photography—History. 2. Daguerre, Louis Jacques Mandé, 1787-1851. 3. Daguerreotype.] I. Title. II. Series.
      TR15.B35 2004
      770'.9--dc22
                                                                                          2003024051
      ISBN 13: 9781584152477

ABOUT THE AUTHOR: Born in Boston, Massachussetts, **John Bankston** began publishing articles in newspapers and magazines while still a teenager. Since then, he has written over two hundred articles, and contributed chapters to books such as *Crimes of Passion*, and *Death Row 2000*, which have been sold in bookstores across the world. He has written numerous biographies for young adults, including *Joseph Lister and the Story of Antiseptics* and *Alexander Graham Bell and the Story of the Telephone* (Mitchell Lane). He currently lives in Portland, Oregon.

PUBLISHER'S NOTE: This story is based on the author's extensive research, which he believes to be accurate. Documentation of such research is contained on page 47.

      The internet sites referenced herein were active as of the publication date. Due to the fleeting nature of some web sites, we cannot guarantee they will all be active when you are reading this book.

                                                                            PLB2,4

Uncharted, Unexplored, and Unexplained

Scientific Advancements of the 19th Century

Louis Daguerre

and the Story of the Daguerreotype

*For Your Information

This portrait of French optician Charles Chevalier (R) sitting with British inventor and physicist Charles Wheatstone was taken around 1843. Chevalier was well-known for his construction of horizontal microscopes. Together with his father Vincent, Charles owned a shop where Louis Daguerre bought all of his lenses.

1

First Photo

The man burst into Charles Chevalier's lens shop. He was out of breath, so excited he could barely speak. "I have found a way of fixing the images of the camera. I have seized the fleeting light and imprisoned it! I have forced the sun to paint pictures for me!"[1]

Slightly overweight with a thick mustache, freckles, and unruly hair, he was a familiar figure at the shop. In the 1830s, Chevalier sold some of the best lenses in Europe. These lenses were used in camera obscuras, devices artists like the excited gentleman used to reflect images for tracing. That day, the gentleman had a breakthrough—but someone seeing him might have thought it was a breakdown.

"Anyone who did not know the man as well as we did, would certainly have believed him to be seized with a fit of madness,"[2] Chevalier admitted many years later in *Guide du Photographie*.

The man wasn't crazy. He was a painter and a showman seeking a way to hold the images he'd seen in the camera obscura. That day he'd gotten a step closer to his dream, but only by accident. He'd left a metal plate coated with silver chloride inside a cupboard of chemicals, and the plate held an image. He didn't know *which* chemical had fixed the image, but the scope of possibilities had been dramatically narrowed.

For decades people constructed complicated contraptions like the camera obscura in an attempt to capture "the fleeting light." Camera obscuras worked by reflecting an upside-down image through a tiny lens and onto a darkened wall. But the pictures faded with the day, and artists had to work quickly to trace them.

People have probably wanted to preserve images from reflected light from the time they first saw themselves in a still pool of water. As with every idea, many claimed it was impossible. Even in the early 1800s, some questioned the science involved in what would become photography, while religious writers argued that since man was made in God's image, capturing a picture of man was like capturing God: impossible to achieve, a sin to attempt.

Louis Daguerre, shown here, was a French painter, known first for his painted stage sets. While he experimented with ways to "paint with light," he was joined in his experiments by Joseph Nicephore Niepce who had been doing related work. They worked together until Niepce's death in 1833. Daguerre completed his invention of the daguerreotype alone.

This 18th century engraving illustrates the use of the camera obscura, the first method artists used to make realistic drawings.

The man who raced into Chevalier's lens shop was not slowed down by the arguments of others. He was too focused on achieving his dream. Not for a second did he think he was defying God. Neither did he worry about whether he was attempting a scientific miracle. After all, he wasn't a scientist. The experiments he conducted had begun with others who owned more scientific knowledge but less time and patience.

Louis Daguerre (dag-AIR) spent most of his life as an artist. He was used to manipulating light and working with the chemicals of his paints. He'd sketched the images from a camera obscura and created some of the most realistic drawings the world had known. In the process he invented the Diorama. In his time it was almost as popular as movie theaters are in ours.

Using the camera obscura, Daguerre created the first photograph. Imagine a world without this discovery. Without photographs there would be no movies, there would be no television. Family photos would be painted portraits. In many cases thousands of words would be needed because pictures would be unavailable.

Daguerre grew up in the shadows of the French Revolution and came of age during an artistic revolution. He lived to see his invention improved and carried into war. He named it after himself. Its story is his story, the story of Louis Daguerre and the daguerreotype.

Revolutionary

Jacques-Louis David

Revolutions can occur in governments. One happened in the United States in 1776 and another in France 13 years later. These revolutions were violent struggles to establish new freedoms within countries.

Revolutions can also occur in art and culture. Although not usually violent, they are just as filled with conflict. In France the artistic styles prior to the 1789 political revolution were very elaborate, such as the excessively ornate rococo style. After the monarchy was overthrown, many different styles competed for attention. New freedoms in politics encouraged new freedoms in art. The rococo style was replaced by more realistic depictions; many artists turned to political paintings. These images reflected both the struggles of the revolution and triumphs of the poor.

Few artists represent the period as well as Jacques-Louis David.

Prior to the revolution, David primarily depicted images from Greek mythology. Utilizing almost photographic realism, his works, which included many nudes, were considered somewhat scandalous in their times.

After 1789, David continued to draw Greek heroes, but he also honored the men and women he considered French heroes, people who had been involved in the uprising. Probably his best-known work, The Death of Marat, shows the murdered body of a man well known for his violent speeches, his corpse lying serenely in his bath.

"The drama is there, alive in all its deplorable horror," wrote the French critic Charles Pierre Baudelaire, ". . . which makes this painting David's masterpiece and one of the great curiosities of modern art, there is nothing trivial or ignoble about it."[3]

By the time David died, his work was not as popular. People were moving into new revolutions. However, his work was resurrected in the 20th century by the cubists, who, although they painted in a very unrealistic style, admired David's precise use of geometry and space to tell a story.

An artist's depiction of the drafting of the Declaration of Independence. This scene in Philadelphia, Pennsylvania took place some eleven years before Louis Daguerre was born near Paris, France.

2

Images in Revolution

When representatives of the 13 British colonies in North America met in Philadelphia, Pennsylvania, in July 1776, their decision would be felt across the world. The Declaration of Independence did more than announce to Britain their intention to govern themselves. It provided a blueprint for many people who lived under the rule of monarchs, kings and queens who gained power through birth, not elections.

In France, King Louis XVI and his wife, Marie-Antoinette, were hugely unpopular with their subjects. "Let them eat cake," she is said to have replied to starving peasants who had no bread. Whether or not she said it, there's no question that the poor and middle classes of France wanted a change. In the late 18th century the line between rich and poor was as solid as concrete and steel, as solid as the Bastille prison which stood as a symbol of the powerlessness of the poor.

In pre-revolutionary France, two systems of justice operated. One was for the rich and well-born, the other for the poor. The Bastille held those unfortunates who were either poor or who opposed the government. For many, imprisonment ended with the sharp blade of the infamous guillotine. This gruesome execution machine beheaded its victims

Marie Antoinette is put on trial in this artist's drawing. Marie Antoinette was born in 1755, one of 16 children of Maria Theresa, the archduchess of Austria and queen of Hungary. Her original name was Maria Antonia. Marie Antoinette was the name she took when she married Louis, the crown prince of France in a marriage arranged by her mother.

with one slice. In 1789, French revolutionaries stormed the prison, freeing those held as much for their beliefs as for any crime.

The French peasants and middle-class subjects demanded freedom— freedom for the political prisoners and freedom to elect their leaders and govern themselves. It was a violent uprising and the streets ran red with blood. The rich and powerful were led to the guillotine, forced to face the same blade they'd once used against the peasants. It was a fate met by both Marie-Antoinette and King Louis XVI.

Meanwhile, as blood and revolution filled the streets of Paris, life went on. People went to work, they fell in love, they got married, they had children. It was, in many ways, "the best of times, . . . the worst of times," as author Charles Dickens wrote in *A Tale of Two Cities*.

That statement was brought to life in the residence of Louis Jacques Daguerre. A crier at the court in Cormeille en Parisis, a rural town near Paris, his job involved announcing the decisions made by the local magistrate, a justice of the peace. In February 1787, he made his own decision when he married 20-year-old Anne Antoinette Hauterre. Just nine months later the couple had a son, and they named him after his father—Louis Jacques Mande Daguerre was born on November 18.

In 18th century France, two systems of justice operated. One was for the rich and well-born, the other for the poor or those who opposed the government. For many of the poor, imprisonment ended at a guillotine like the one shown here.

Louis Sr. didn't want any part of the revolution. He was a royalist—someone who supported the royal family—and when he and his wife had a daughter in 1791, he named her Marie Antoinette.

Around this time, Louis Sr. accepted a position as a clerk at the royal estates in Orléans, where he and his family relocated. When he was old enough, little Louis began attending school nearby.

Going to a public school like the one Louis attended was a difficult business in the 1790s. The revolution was focused on social change, but school funding didn't seem to be at the top of the list. Teachers weren't paid, so they didn't show up for work, and with few educators available, neither did the students. One survey conducted in a Parisian school district showed that out of 21,000 school-age children, barely 1,000 continued attending classes.

Louis was one of the few who did attend, and despite the challenges of inadequate materials, crowded classes, and unreliable teachers, he still managed to learn. Much of his talent he brought to school with him.

From the first time he held a pen or a brush, Louis could draw pictures that were far more realistic than could the other kids his age. The world he saw—the gated estates of Orléans, the streets of Paris, the rural countryside—all were part of his illustrations.

At 13, Louis proved his skill to his parents by drawing their portrait. They were astonished. Louis Sr. also had an idea. A boy with his son's ability might go far with the right job, and he arranged for Louis to apprentice to an architect. Although he was barely a teenager, in the 18th century he was at the right age to think about a career. An apprenticeship, though it would pay little or nothing, would be an opportunity to learn a profession.

In 1801, Louis took a position that would teach him how to be a draftsman for an architect. In some ways the job was great training for an artist. It improved his realistic style: when he drew the lines of planned buildings, he needed to be incredibly accurate. It also taught him about perspective—how to make two-dimensional objects appear to have depth and distance from the viewer, the way a winding road in a painting can appear to stretch forever. It was a good tool for a budding architect to have in his shed. Ultimately, however, Louis didn't want to be an architect. He wanted to be an artist.

Louis Sr. was convinced his son was crazy. For him, art was not a profession; it was not a job. Artists starved. The few lucky ones made a meager living as portrait painters. Louis held his ground—he wanted to go to Paris, which to him was the center of all things artistic.

In the end father and son compromised. Louis could go to Paris, but he would still have to learn a skilled trade. He would apprentice again, this time under Ignace Eugene Marie Degotti, a stage designer at the Paris Opera. Because of his father's worries, Louis would live with Degotti and work in his studio.

Degotti was well-known in the theater community, his sets were striking in their realism and imagination. For Louis it was a chance to combine his creative side with the precision he'd gained working for the architect. Crafting backdrops for the stage, he had to make sure that each object looked exactly like its real-life counterpart. He had to apply perspective so that the audience would accept the illusions of distances.

Despite Louis Sr.'s precautions, his son was only 16 years old, and he behaved like most teenagers alone in a big city. He went a little bit wild. It was easy for him to make friends with the actors and actresses who worked at the Paris Opera and other nearby theaters. Many of them had well-deserved reputations for outrageous behavior.

Besides his labors designing sets, Louis also appeared in a number of shows as a dancer. He even managed some tightrope walking. Socially he could always be counted on to participate in one of the dances that were extremely popular in the early 1800s. Sometimes he'd arrive at these parties upside down, walking in on his hands. Of course, considering the group he hung out with, this was barely noticed.

After spending several years in the theater, Louis decided he needed a new challenge. A popular art form was sweeping Europe, and he wanted to be involved. Called panorama, it was as popular then as movies would be a century later. It also would set Louis on the path to discovering a process that would someday make movies possible.

During the 1920s, music and dance married into a decade often called the jazz age. Even those who don't recognize the names of dances like the Charleston and the jitterbug are probably familiar with their wild leg movements and almost acrobatic skill. The early 1800s had its own dance and music craze, and its movements are familiar to anyone who has seen movies set in that era.

One of the most popular dances was the English country dance. As its name suggests, it originated in England, but it quickly spread across Europe and into the United States. Indeed, dance fanatics in the United States waited eagerly, lining up to buy new books of steps.

In France, where Louis Daguerre was enjoying his youth, English country dance steps had been first detailed in 1710s Recueil de Contredanse, which showed readers a variety of the dance's moves and changes. By the early 1800s, the dance had become complicated, while another version of it, the quadrille, grew even more popular.

Both the English country dance and the quadrille had couples moving in precise arrangements, changing partners or steps regularly—often at the instruction of a caller. The music they listened to had been written especially for English country dances by some of the top writers of the time—composers like Wolfgang Amadeus Mozart and Ludwig van Beethoven.

The quadrille relied on four couples moving through five different figures, a dance routine that required coordination and rhythm along with a fair level of athletic ability. By all accounts, teenage Louis Daguerre was a natural. He was a great hit at ballrooms and was often invited to the garden cafés, where patrons moved through more casual forms of the dance.

This is an artist's conception of Louis Daguerre's diorama.

3

A New Excitement

Imagine sitting in a darkened room, staring at a picture. The picture doesn't move, the subjects do nothing. The most impressive part is the realism of the image and the way the overhead light dances across the painting. Your seat moves from one painting to the next. You've paid your admission, and so you sit there, watching. No matter how beautiful the paintings were, the attraction was like going to an art gallery with mobile seats.

Sound boring? Well consider that in the early 1800s, there were of course no movies and no TV. Live theater and other staged performances were just about the only other entertainment option you could get a ticket to. All other forms—playing piano or reading, for example—took place in the home.

First demonstrated by Robert Barker in 1787, the panorama consisted of very large paintings hung in a theater setting. The most impressive of these panoramas was over 300 feet long and 45 feet high. Despite their size, each detail had to be precisely drawn. In fact, some audience members even tried to reach out and touch the painting, certain that the grass was real, the water wet.

Drawing a panorama required an artist's eye and a draftsman's precision. Louis Daguerre was perfect for the job. Like a college student switching majors, Louis took a job in 1807 as an assistant. This decision could only have worried his parents; at 20 he'd reached the age where a young man was expected to be earning his own way in the world. Instead he was working for low wages as he tried to master yet another profession.

Still, if he wanted to become the best at panorama, apprenticing to Pierre Prevost would be a great place to start. "Really one has to come here to study nature,"[1] the painter Jacques-Louis David was heard telling one of his pupils at a Prevost panorama. Indeed, Prevost's work was more than just a duplication of the outside world, it was an im-provement.

Socially, young Louis's life was changing as well. Sometime after he began apprenticing to Prevost, he also began dating Louise Georgina Smith. The daughter of English parents, she'd grown up near Paris. She was 20 years old when she and Louis married on November 10, 1810.

Although he'd found a potentially interesting profession and a woman who loved him, Louis had far less luck reaching his original dream. He painted in his spare time, but there wasn't much spare time in his life. He'd managed to paint only a half dozen or so works in nearly two decades. None of these paintings were well reviewed, nor did they sell well. What they had going for them was realism, and as Louis grew older the concept of realistically depicting life became more and more fascinating.

In 1816 he returned to the world of stage design, getting his first decent-paying job at the Théâtre de l'Ambigu-Comique. Almost 30, he must have wondered if the ambitions he'd had as a kid were just a waste of time.

The theater was a great place to experiment. It had grown from a stuffy institution favored by the rich to a rollicking spectacle popular with the middle and working classes. Louis designed sets that reflected the theater's new audience, incorporating elaborate lighting, carefully crafted illusions, and stage effects. He also completely redecorated the theater using an enormous blue drapery as a curtain.

Louis spent two years at the opera, and his designs for *Aladdin*, with the genie's wonderful lamp, met with special praise from local critics: "Never has the opera offered the public a more magnificent and elegant spectacle . . . there are ten new decorations which do honor to Ciceri and Daguerre,"[2] reported the *Miroir de Spectacles*.

But Louis wanted to do more than design theater sets and work on panoramas for others. He wanted to create his own designs, his own entertainment, something that would marry the spectacle of live theater with the realistic depictions of panorama. Combining the Greek words for "through" (*dia*) and "view" (*horama*), he named it diorama, because audiences would be treated to realistic illustrations on a screen thin enough to see through.

Beginning in 1822, he and his friend from Prevost's Panorama, C. M. Bouton, opened the first diorama entertainment. Many believe the pair were inspired by the diaphorama made famous by artist Franz Konig. While Konig's work was meant to be viewed as art, Bouton and Daguerre hoped to offer their work as both art *and* entertainment.

The diorama (like the diaphorama) involved a painted screen with a very realistic illustration. The diorama added lighting effects, so if the painting required sunlight, there was a lamp substituting for it over the painting. It also added songs—like a movie sound track, these paintings incorporated appropriate music with the scene.

Bouton and Daguerre did more than just improve on the original with lighting and music, they also developed a brand-new way for the audience to watch the show. Instead of the audience going to the paintings, the paintings went to them.

Patrons were ushered down a dim corridor, lit only by shaded floor lamps, and into a darkened room. As they stepped forward, their eyes adjusted and portions of the painting would come into view. Some objects seemed three-dimensional. Some patrons were so fooled by the display, they reached forward to touch it. Others wadded up paper and tossed it at the "water" to see a splash.

Once the entire audience was inside the room and had an opportunity to look at the illustration, the floor moved, bringing the next diorama to them. Constructed on sliding rails with a single pivot in the center, the diorama was similar to a carousel, and its entire movement was controlled by one person who operated a crank at the sound of a bell.

The diorama was fairly high priced entertainment, charging two francs to stand on the floor and three to sit in the amphitheater. This was much more than a ticket to the theater, but the diorama consistently sold out.

It was also very well reviewed: "The representation of water flowing down a small and slight declivity is so perfectly natural as to impress an observer with the conviction that the artist has created, by some ingenious mechanism, to let real water issue from an aperture made in part of the canvas,"[3] offered a writer from the *Journal de Paris* in 1822. Another with the *Miroir des Spectacles* wrote, "Never has any representation of nature struck me so vividly."[4]

The show did so well that in 1823 Bouton was able to open the diorama in Regents Park, London. The next year he and Daguerre took out a patent in England on the project. Then no one else would be able to copy it without their permission.

But by then, Daguerre wanted other challenges. He had changed the way people viewed art, combining paintings with theater. Soon he'd be seeking a patent for a discovery that would change not only the way people viewed art, but the way they looked at life itself.

"Our boxes and orchestras are now occupied almost exclusively by shop girls, apprentice locksmiths and market porters who come to kill time and not infrequently to display their jewels,"[5] complained a disgusted gentleman in an issue of Le Decade published in the 1790s.

Theater censorship had ended in 1791. Suddenly playwrights were free to create stories about murder, adultery, and other seedy subjects they'd once been warned away from. The theater audience had once been exclusively noble or upper class; now it included people from all types of backgrounds, and they were hungry for the kinds of stories that today would be seen on afternoon soap operas.

Of all the writers, few were as popular as René-Charles Guilbert de Pixérécourt. A child of a well-connected family, he barely escaped death in the French Revolution. During his career he wrote 120 plays, which were performed over 30,000 times. In the early 1800s a play performed 100 times was considered a success.

He wrote, it was said, for people who did not read. Since illiteracy rates skyrocketed after the revolution, his audience was very large indeed.

Many of Pixérécourt's plays were performed at the Théâtre de l'Ambigu-Comique, where Louis Daguerre was a stage designer. The theater sat on the boulevard du Temple, often called boulevard du crime because of the many plays that featured murders in their storylines.

This portrait of French photographic pioneer, Louis Daguerre, was painted around 1830.

4

The Origins of Light Writing

Humans have re-created their world in mud and clay for thousands of years. The need to tell the stories of their lives and reimagine the world in which they lived predates the written word. Still, the journey to producing an image that exactly duplicates something in nature was a very long one.

It was sometime in 500 B.C. when Mo Ti noticed the way light could reflect off an object, travel through a pinhole, and then be seen to re-create the object on a darkened wall. Although it would take over two thousand years, that discovery in China paved the way for modern photography.

Since the pinhole Mo Ti was looking through was probably fairly large, the resulting image would have been faint and blurry.

It would also have been upside down, as all images reflected through a pinhole are.

Eventually this led to camera obscuras, darkened rooms designed to "capture" the outside world through a pinhole reflection. An artist could sit in the darkened room and trace an image. The result was a very realistic painting. By 1560, Danielo Barbado added a lens to the pinhole, and this greatly improved the quality of the reflected image.

It also improved the accuracy of the resulting portrait, and the camera obscura became a tool not just for artists but also for draftsmen, architects, and anyone else who needed a picture that was as close as possible to the original.

The problem was, relying on a darkened room limited the mobility of the camera obscura. Some substituted a darkened tent for a darkened room, but these were still unwieldy.

Finally in the 1700s, improvements in the camera obscura's design and the shape of its lens reduced its size to a small darkened box—not terribly different from the cameras that would follow them a century later.

As the 18th century bled into the 19th, the science of preserving an image took a tremendous leap forward. It wasn't a scientist who made the discovery. The man was a British china maker named Thomas Wedgwood. In 1799, he began to refine the process of "capturing" an image.

Wedgwood had just received an order from Russia—Czarina Catherine the Great wanted over 1,000 table services: bowls, cups, plates, etcetera. It was a huge order, and her precise instructions that they each have pictures of gardens, landscapes, and the rural manor houses England is famous for made the order even more demanding. Rushed for time, Wedgwood began with a camera obscura but decided to see if he could produce one image and then use chemicals to preserve and transfer it. He'd read up on work done with silver salts for similar purposes, so he used a combination of sunlight and nitrates to place an image. "On being exposed to daylight, [the image] speedily changes color," he later wrote, "and after passing through different shades of grays and browns becomes at length newly black."[1]

Portrait of Catherine II of Russia (1729-1796). She ordered 1,000 table services from Thomas Wedgwood, who in 1799, began to refine his process of "capturing" images to put them on his china.

Unfortunately the images he created faded quickly and were of little use in filling the czarina's order.

In 1826, Joseph-Nicéphore Niepce managed to produce an image that lasted. He took a metal plate covered in a substance called bitumen of Judea and put it inside a camera obscura. Then he aimed the camera through a window and waited.

And waited.

Hours later, he removed the plate, dunked it in a bath of oil solvent to remove the extra bitumen, and took a look. The image left behind was a near duplicate to what he could see outside his window. He called his new invention a heliograph, after the Greek word *helio*, for "sun," and *graph*, for "writing."

French chemist Joseph Nicephore Niepce (1765 - 1833), inventor of the photochemical process on metal in 1826. Niepce worked with Daguerre on the photographic process until his death in 1833.

The discovery was amazing but not very practical. It took far too long for a picture to be made. No one was going to stand around motionless for several hours while their picture was recorded. Also, the image that resulted lacked the shadows and light we're familiar with in modern pictures.

It took an artist's imagination to solve a scientific dilemma. Louis Daguerre was familiar with the camera obscura; he'd used one in making panoramas and dioramas. Since very precise, realistic pictures were important in both entertainments, it's easy to see why he used it.

Louis's motives for pursuing what would become photography are less clear. Like many, he may have wanted to hold an image forever, instead of having the fleeting representations created by the camera obscura. Besides, a photograph could speed up the process of diorama production. However, it was the idea that photography might produce a new form of entertainment which probably motivated Daguerre the most. He was, after all, a businessman as much as he was an artist.

Regardless of his motivations, he'd soon forget about the diorama altogether. Beginning in 1826, he began writing to Niepce about his

This is the world's first photograph taken by Joseph Niepce. It was taken from a window of his Le Gras estate at Saint-Loup-de-Varennes, France. It was produced by exposing a bitumen-coated pewter plate in a camera obscura. It took an exposure time of eight hours.

experiments, and in 1829 the two formed an important partnership, with the older Frenchman supplying the science and Louis supplying everything else.

It could have been a challenging partnership. Niepce was reserved and aristocratic, whereas Louis was wilder. He'd hounded the older inventor for years before they finally met. Part of the reason Louis wanted him for a partner was he feared that Niepce was further along than he was in his experiments.

He was probably right.

Niepce wondered about Louis's scientific abilities, but he never questioned his artistic talent after seeing his greatest invention so far. "I have seen nothing here that has struck me more or given me more pleasure than the diorama,"[2] he said.

The diorama followed the other things in Louis's life. As he became more obsessed with his photography experiments, everything else became less important. His friends worried about his health, his wife worried about his sanity, but like most scientists and inventors struck by an idea, Louis just couldn't let it go.

Niepce had contributed the idea of a silver plate inside the camera obscura, and Chevalier provided the lens. Daguerre would begin to use metal in the camera obscura, slowly transforming it into the camera we're familiar with today. He also inserted a mirror to flip the upside-down image. The result was a mirror image of the subject. The hardest part for Daguerre was discovering the right set of chemicals to properly "expose" the image.

Niepce's health began to fail. His death in 1833 left Louis to conduct the chemical experiments himself. He had a barely adequate education and little training in chemistry. He turned to the textbooks of the time, including the eight-volume *Treatise on Chemistry*, which included a list of over 100 light-sensitive chemicals.

Mostly it was trial and error for Louis. He was probably lucky he didn't accidentally poison himself or blow up his house.

Sometime between 1831 and 1835, Daguerre discovered that light hitting carbonic acid gas in combination with iodine produced a very faint image. He also recognized that chlorate of potassium heated using a lamp inside a closed box produced color in the iodine.

The word *photograph* comes from the Greek words *photos,* for "light," and *graphos,* for "writing," and that is what Louis was trying to do. He was trying to write with light. It was an exasperating process, adding chemicals to the silver plate to see which ones would reduce the exposure time. Unfortunately all the shades of color he produced were horrible, and the images were too flawed to even consider.

But he knew if he found the right chemical to add to the silver plate, he'd have a photograph.

The story of how he discovered that chemical is widely related, but no one is certain whether or not it is true. The tale goes that one fine spring day he neglected to remove an underexposed silver plate from his cupboard of chemicals. When he woke up the next morning and opened the cupboard, he discovered a clear picture on the plate.

It was astonishing. One of the many chemicals inside his cupboard had done the trick. But which one? There was only one way to find out. So again, Louis had to rely on trial and error as he tested each chemical against a batch of underexposed silver plates. After a very long time he realized that the chemical came not form his stores, but from a broken thermometer. The mercury had leaked out and the gas had "developed" his picture. It was just the breakthrough Louis needed.

In *La Photographie Consideree Comme Art et Comme Industrie,* Louis admitted his feelings about the discovery: "The many preceding disappointments had depressed me so much that I was no longer capable of feeling excited about it. You must not forget that this discovery only happened after eleven years of discouraging experiments which had damped my spirits."[3]

Adding a chemical vapor to produce a picture from the silver-coated plate was just the first step toward making a photograph. Developing the picture brought out the light; after more experimentation, Daguerre realized that bathing the plate in a solution of hyposulfite of soda made the image endure and eliminated its light sensitivity. In other words, it "stopped" the exposure and "fixed" the image.

After rinsing the plate in water, he protected the image with an elaborate brass frame. Inside a booklike case lined with velvet or silk, the mirror image was striking in its detail. Paintings become less distinct under a magnifying glass, but Daguerre's images grew sharper.

The process of adding chemicals to an exposed image to produce a picture has only changed in the specifics, but is very similar to darkroom photo processing today.

Louis Daguerre was so proud of the process, he named it after himself, marketing it as the daguerreotype. In a few short years everyone from U.S. President Abraham Lincoln and writer Edgar Allen Poe to everyday people would have one done of themselves. First, though, Louis had to figure out a way to make money from it.

Gets Shot—On Film

American writer Edgar Allan Poe invented many characters who use shadows and subterfuge to escape detection. Considered by many to be the first great writer of both detective and horror fiction, Poe was an unlikely subject for a device that required as much light as it did darkness.

Edgar Allan Poe

Poe's motives for having his portrait done were probably the same as many writers' motives to write: to leave something of themselves behind after they die. When he walked into the photo studio of S. W. Hartshorn, Poe was coming to the end of what had been a hard and tragic life. Orphaned as a toddler, disowned by the man who raised him, and kicked out of West Point, in 1847 he buried his wife Virginia Clemm, whom he'd married when she was 13.

When he had his portrait made in 1848, Poe probably figured there was little chance anyone would remember him for his fiction. He'd made only a meager living as an author, and future literary success seemed unlikely.

Poe's portrait shows a ghostly man, his gaunt face looking at least a decade older than his 39 years, possibly due in part to his drinking and drug habits. His vest is haphazardly buttoned and lies open in the center, his hair is messy and slick. It is the best picture we have of the man.

"If we examine a work of ordinary art by means of a powerful microscope, all traces of resemblance to nature will disappear," he is quoted in the book The Keepers of Light, "but the closest scrutiny of the daguerreotype discloses only a more absolute truth, a more perfect identity of aspect with the thing represented."[4]

The year after his picture was made, Poe died. Since then, his books have become widely loved, and his picture remains, preserving an author whose demons seem forever captured by the daguerreotype.

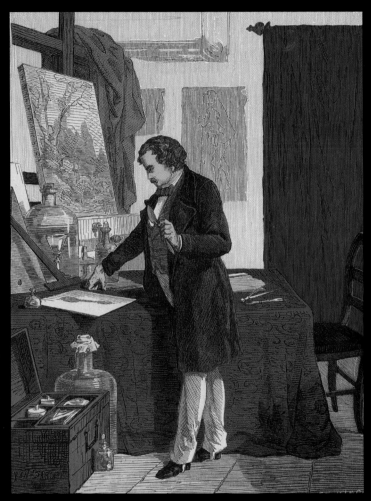

This illustration shows Louis Daguerre at work. He is shown here discovering the light-sensitive properties of silver iodide. A spoon in his hand is casting a shadow on the card at center left, forming an image. Although originally employed as a tax officer, Daguerre became a painter of opera scenery, and invented the illuminated diorama. After this he started work on chemicals sensitive to light. Daguerre unveiled the Daguerreotype in 1839.

5

Another Type of Picture

Having discovered something he was sure would change the world, Louis Daguerre needed only one thing: money. Even as he sought to find buyers for his invention, he fought with the son of the man who'd helped him invent it. Isidore Niepce refused to sign papers admitting that Louis was responsible for the invention of the daguerreotype, nor would he agree to just market his father's earlier, slower process.

It was easy to argue both sides of the issue. Joseph Niepce discovered part of the process that led to Daguerre's breakthroughs, but he'd used the wrong chemicals. Only the younger man's arduous experiments led to the final product. The dispute was complicated, but for Louis not as complicated as finding an income.

In an attempt to develop interest in the daguerreotype, Louis took his invention to the streets of Paris. Behind him he lugged a cart loaded with nearly 100 pounds of equipment—the "portable" means to produce a single photograph. With an exposure time of nearly 20 minutes, he mainly shot buildings and alleyways; people seemed to disappear, as movement erased their images. However, his early work produced his most famous image, a man unaware he was being photographed having

This is Louis Jacques Daguerre's first surviving daguerreotype image. It is of a collection of plaster casts on a window ledge, which he produced on a silver plate around 1837.

his shoes shined. This man, who was relatively motionless for long enough for his image to appear, was probably the first person ever photographed. Although there was also a man shining his shoes, the motion of the shoe shiner was too fast to capture.

The images struck reviewers who saw them, like the writer for Boston's daily *Advertiser*, who noted several years later that the daguerreotype "reproduces the freshness of morning—the brilliancy of noon—the dim twilight and dullness of a rainy day."[1]

In order to attract sponsors, Louis had his own positive words for the invention. It "consists," he said, "in the spontaneous reproduction of the images of nature received in the camera obscura, not with colors faded but with very fine graduations of tones." He hoped his few words and pictures would entice at least 400 subscribers to pay 1,000 francs each to own one of his inventions. Subscriptions would also include the instructions to make it work. He promised, as practically all inventors do, that his device was so easy to use, anyone could operate it.

Daguerre found few buyers. To the general public his device seemed like an illusion, part of a well-produced magic act. Fortunately for Daguerre, scientists and politicians weren't so skeptical. He brought it along to numerous meetings, and one scientist in particular became the unwieldy contraption's champion.

François Arago was the director of the Paris Observatory and a leader in the political body called the Chamber of Deputies. He was a good friend for Louis to have. He quickly realized the daguerreotype's potential, and he believed that associating it with the French people rather than just a single citizen would do his country good. So instead of helping Louis sell it to the public, he helped him sell it to France.

On Monday, January 7, 1839, Arago presented Daguerre's invention and the pictures he'd taken with it to the Academy of Sciences. They

Portrait of François Arago, the French physicist and astronomer. Arago showed that metals other than iron could have magnetic properties; he also discovered that an electric current produces a magnetic field. In 1838 he devised an experiment to prove the wave nature of light by comparing its speed in air and water; this was performed successfully by Foucault in 1850.

agreed with Arago, and shortly thereafter the French government paid Daguerre several thousand francs and a lifetime pension. In exchange they would release it for free to the world. Unfortunately, by the time that happened eight months later, a similar invention had been patented in England, and, as Lady Elizabeth Eastlake, wife of Charles Eastlake, President of the Royal Photographic Society, noted, "for a time rendered [England] the only country which did not benefit by the liberality of the French government."

The British had another claim besides the patent. William Henry Talbot's experiments with Calotypes occurred nearly simultaneously as the daguerreotype's debut. However, Calotypes were not as clear or as attractive, so they never gained favor. Talbot refused to give up, demonstrating just as much determination as Daguerre had. His work led to the photo negative, an important step toward photo portability.

After receiving his pension and retiring to Bry-Sur-Marne, Daguerre didn't end his own experiments. Working with the lens, he designed a device that could shut out as much or as little light as the photographer wanted—the first shutter. He also wrote books describing the best ways to create a daguerreotype.

Daguerre lived long enough to see his device embraced by millions. Across the world, daguerreotype studios opened up, as his camera was used to capture portraits in peacetime and battle scenes in warfare. He lived a quiet life with his wife, remaining active in the photography community. On July 10, 1851, while eating lunch, the normally healthy Louis Daguerre commented that he felt ill. A moment later he collapsed. Less than an hour later he was dead of an apparent heart attack.

Louis Daguerre's legacy has outlived him, not only in the pictures he took, but in the picture taken of him, still preserved over 150 years later. The sepia-toned pictures he developed led to the images we see today, on movies, on television, and in family snapshots. Even in our modern world there are still daguerreotype enthusiasts, producing pictures just as he did.

War Photographer

Mathew Brady was still a teenager when in the 1840s he embraced the new technology of photography. Having been taught the technique by Samuel Morse, Brady was able to open his own studio by the time he was 21 years old. He soon developed the kind of fame usually reserved for people who have their pictures taken, not for those behind the camera.

Mathew Brady

"The fact that Mathew Brady sought you out to take your picture meant that you were news. You could be notorious or interesting or famous. You need not necessarily be good or great," one writer remembers in the book *L.J.M. Daguerre*. Soon Brady was both well off and well known. He decided to risk it all when the United States plunged into the Civil War in 1860.

Brady abandoned his lucrative portrait business in order to capture the conflict's reality with his camera. Until then images from wars were painted long after the battles ended. They were seldom realistic depictions.

Brady assembled a team of top cameramen who fanned out across the country. The pictures they took were

unique and chilling. Although Brady himself took few of them, his name appears on the credits because of his work organizing and conducting the team. In some ways he was more like a movie director of today than a cameraman, except of course the "actors" were soldiers and the conflict was very real.

"The terrible reality and earnestness of war" is how The New York Times described perhaps the most chilling image to come out of Brady's efforts. Entitled *The Dead of Antietam*, it shows bodies lying in the aftermath of the battle. It shocked the nation and preserved Brady's reputation for history.

It also cost Brady every penny he had. After the war he never recovered from the debts he accumulated. He died in 1896, broke and alone.

Chronology

1787	Born on November 18 to Louis-Jacques Daguerre and Anne Antoinette Hauterre in Cormeille en Parisis, France
1792	Begins attending the Orléans public school
1801	Apprentices with architect in Orléans
1804	Apprentices with the stage designer of the Paris Opera, Ignace Degotti
1807	Becomes an assistant to Pierre Prevost in panorama painting
1810	Marries Louise Georgina Smith
1814	Exhibits his first painting at the Salon
1816	Becomes a designer at the Théâtre de l'Ambigu-Comique
1819	Becomes a designer at the Paris Opera
1822	Working with C. M. Bouton, opens the diorama in Paris
1823	Opens the diorama at Regents Park in London, England
1824	Begins photographic experiments
1825	Receives the Cross of the Legion of Honour
1826	Writes his first letter to Nicéphore Niepce, the inventor of heliography
1827	Meets with Niepce
1829	Becomes a partner with Niepce in experiments with photography
1830	Ends partnership with Bouton
1833	After Niepce dies, becomes partner with Niepce's son, Isidore
1834	Collaborating with Hippolyte Sebron, produces his first double-effect diorama
1835	After discovering the development of latent image using mercury vapor, he alters contract with Isidore Niepce
1837	Uses common table salt to "fix" the image
1839	Along with Isidore Niepce, unsuccessfully tries to gain subscribers for daguerreotype; the invention is announced at France's Academy of Sciences; French government purchases daguerreotype; Daguerre, along with Niepce, receives pension for process

Chronology (Cont'd)

1840   Retires at Bry-sur-Marne

1851   Dies of a heart attack on July 10

Timeline of Discovery

500 B.C   Mo Ti observes that when light is reflected from an object and the reflection passes through a pinhole onto a darkened surface, an upside-down picture of the object is produced.

1000   Ibn Al-Haitham discovers that when the pinhole is smaller, the reflected image is clearer.

1490   Leonardo da Vinci describes the camera obscura.

1560   Italian Danielo Barbado uses a lens in place of just a pinhole, greatly improving image quality.

1700s   Camera obscura, a tentlike room that enables artists to view pinhole reflections, is reduced to the portable size of a small box with the addition of a magnifying lens and ground glass.

1727   Johann H. Schulze demonstrates light sensitivity of silver salts.

1735–68   Artist Giovanni Canaletto improves the lens to a "flat field lens," improving picture quality even more.

1802   Thomas Wedgwood develops a chemical solution that briefly "fixes" an image.

1816   Joseph-Nicéphore Niepce combines photosensitive paper with a camera obscura; he creates a permanent image in 1829.

1837   The daguerreotype is introduced.

1841   Talbot patents his Calotype.

1847   Claude Felix Abel Niepce de Saint-Victor shows that albumen (egg white) is a successful coating for the glass photo plate.

1851   Englishman Frederick Archer uses collodion to reduce exposure time to between twenty seconds and two minutes.

Timeline of Discovery (Cont'd)

1854   Adolphe Disdéri develops carte-de-visite photos in Paris, sparking an explosion in the number of portrait studios.

1871   A photographic dry plate is introduced.

1888   George Eastman introduces small and portable Kodak camera.

1887   Thomas Alva Edison commissions W.K.L. Dickson to invent a motion picture camera.

1888   First motion picture films are made on sensitized paper rolls taken with a camera by Louis Aime Augustin Le Prince.

1889   Improved Kodak camera features roll of film instead of paper.

1894   *Edison Kinetoscopic Record of a Sneeze, January 7, 1894*, is filmed at a motion picture studio, nicknamed "Black Maria," that rotates on tracks to follow the light of the sun. The studio was built by Edison in West Orange, New Jersey.

1895   Max and Emil Skladanowsky shows a 15-minute public program of films in Berlin.

1897   American Mutoscope, owned by Herman Casler and W.K.L. Dickson, is the most popular film company in the United States.

1899   Pathé-Frères, the world's largest film producer and distributor through World War I, is founded.

1900   Kodak Brownie box roll-film camera is produced.

1902   Alfred Stieglitz organizes the Photo-Secession Group in New York City. 1932—Technicolor film is introduced into motion picture photography.

1963   Polaroid introduces the first color instant film.

1990   Kodak announces development of the photo CD system; introduces digital camera a year later.

2003   Greater need for security in the United Sates and around the world creates growing demand for advanced camera technology, including facial recognition cameras, supersensitive X-ray machines, and retina scans.

Chapter Notes

Chapter One: First Photo

1. Helmut and Alison Gernsheim, *L.J.M. Daguerre: The History of the Diorama and the Daguerreotype,* (New York: Dover Publications, 1968), p. 51.

2. Ibid.

3. Sophie Monnert, *David and Neoclassicism,* (Paris: Bayard Presse, SA, 1999), p. 111.

Chapter Three: A New Excitement

1. Helmut and Alison Gernsheim, *L.J.M. Daguerre: The History of the Diorama and the Daguerreotype,* (New York: Dover Publications, 1968), p. 7.

2. Ibid., p. 12.

3. Ibid., p. 19.

4. Ibid., p. 18.

5. Frederick Brown, *Theatre and Revolution: The Culture of the French Stage,* (New York: Viking Press, 1980), p. 84.

Chapter Four: The Origins of Light Writing

1. Alma Davenport, *The History of Photography,* (Boston: Local Press, 1991), p. 6.

2. Helmut and Alison Gernsheim, *L.J.M. Daguerre: The History of the Diorama and the Daguerreotype,* (New York: Dover Publications, 1968), p. 57.

3. Ibid., p. 72.

4. William Crawford, *The Keepers of Light: A History and Working Guide to Early Photographic Processes,* (New York: Morgan and Morgan, 1980) p. 28.

Chapter Five: Another Type of Picture

1. David Weil and Denise M. Bonilla, eds., *Leaders of the Information Age,* (New York: H.W. Wilson, 2003), p. 44.

Glossary

diorama (die eh RAH ma)—a miniature three-dimensional scene.

expose subject photographic plates or film to light.

guillotine (GIH leh teen)—a machine with a heavy blade that falls vertically, used to execute people by beheading them.

negative a photographic image in which the light and dark areas are opposite of those in the original subject.

panorama (pan ah RAH ma)—A picture that unrolls in front of the viewer.

perspective (per SPEK tiv)—a drawing or painting technique to give the illusion of depth and distance.

For Further Reading

For Young Adults:

Coe, Brian. *George Eastman and the Early Photographers.* London: Priory Press, 1973.

Gaines, Ann. *American Photographers: Capturing the Image.* Berkeley Heights, N.J.: Enslow Publishers, 2002.

Jackson, Nancy. *Photographers: History and Culture Through the Camera.* New York: Facts on File, 1997.

Mitchell, Barbara. *CLICK!: A Story about George Eastman.* Minneapolis: Carolrhoda Books, 2003.

Pflueger, Lynda. *George Eastman: Bringing Photography to the People.* Berkeley Heights, N.J.: Enslow Publishers, 2002.

Sandler, Martin W. *Photography: An Illustrated History.* New York: Oxford University Press, 2002.

Sullivan, George. *Black Artists in Photography, 1840–1940.* New York: Cobblehill Books, 1996.

———. *Mathew Brady: His Life and Photographs.* New York: Cobblehill Books, 1994.

Works Consulted:

Brown, Frederick. *Theatre and Revolution: The Culture of the French Stage.* New York: Viking Press, 1980.

Crawford, William. *The Keepers of Light: A History and Working Guide to Early Photographic Processes.* New York: Morgan and Morgan, 1980.

Davenport, Alma. *The History of Photography.* Boston: Focal Press, 1991.

Gernsheim, Helmut and Alison. *L.J.M. Daguerre: The History of the Diorama and the Daguerreotype.* New York: Dover Publications, 1968.

Monnert, Sophie. *David and Neo-Classicism.* Paris: Bayard Presse SA, 1999.

Richter, Stefan. *The Art of the Daguerreotype.* London: Penguin Group, 1989.

Weil, David and Denise M. Bonilla, eds. *Leaders of the Information Age.* New York: H. W. Wilson, 2003.

Wood, John, editor. *America and the Daguerreotype.* Iowa City: University of Iowa Press, 1991.

On the Web:

Mathew Brady
   http://www.american
   strategy.org/bios/mbrady.html

The Daguerreian Society
   http://www.daguerre.org

English Country Dance and Its American Cousin
   http://www-
   ssrl.slac.stanford.edu/
   ~winston/ecd/history.htmlx

George Eastman House Timeline of Photography
   http://www.eastman.org/
   5_timeline/5_index.html

Louis Jacques Mande Daguerre
   http://www.rleggat.com/
   photohistory/history/
   daguerr.htm

Poe, Edgar Allan
   http://bau2.uibk.ac.at/sg/poe/
   Bio.html

Index